Farm Babies

Farm Babies

RUSSELL FREEDMAN

Holiday House · New York

Photo Credits: Page 2, USDA Photo by Gordon Baer; 6-7, 13, 18, USDA Photos; 8, 10, 11, Jerome Wexler/Photo Researchers; 14, 26, Joe Munroe/Photo Researchers; 16, 17, 20, 21, Elizabeth McBride-Smith; 22, Carl Koski/Photo Researchers; 24, C. P. Fox/Photo Researchers; 25, Barbara Young, M.D./Photo Researchers; 27, C. G. Maxwell/Photo Researchers; 29, Pierre Berger/Photo Researchers; 30, Robert E. Brown/Photo Researchers; 32, Mary Eleanor Browning/Photo Researchers; 34, 35, Karl H. Maslowski/Photo Researchers; 36, 39, Gordon S. Smith/Photo Researchers.

Library of Congress Cataloging in Publication Data

Freedman, Russell.
  Farm babies.

  Summary: Describes the offspring of eleven familiar
farm animals including a calf, piglet, and foal.
    1. Domestic animals—Juvenile literature. 2. Animals,
Infancy of—Juvenile literature. [1. Domestic animals.
2. Animals—Infancy] I. Title.
SF75.5.F67   636'.07   81.2898
ISBN 0-8234-0426-9   AACR2

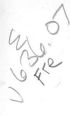

To Daisy Wallace and her friends

Spring is a busy time on the farm. In the pond, frogs are laying their eggs. In the barn, a swallow is building her nest. All over the farm, animals are ready to give birth to their young.

This calf was just born. Its fur is still wet.

Its mother bends down to lick it. She licks the calf clean and smooths its fur with her tongue. And she keeps sniffing it. She'll be able to tell her own calf from all the others by its special smell.

The calf lies quietly in the grass, drying off in the sun. In a moment, it will try to stand up.

Standing up is hard work. The legs of a new calf are long and weak and wobbly. Its mother can't help. The calf must stand by itself. At last it gets to its feet. Fifteen minutes after being born, it is standing on all fours.

Now that it's on its feet, the calf feels hungry. It sniffs its mother's belly, searching for a nipple. The cow nudges the calf. Finally it finds the right place. The cow's udder is filled with warm milk, and the calf begins to suck.

At first a calf needs milk from its own mother, or from another cow that has just given birth. Mother's milk is both food and medicine. It has the vitamins a calf needs, and it protects the calf from getting sick. After a few days, a calf can drink milk that comes from any cow in the herd.

The calves shown here are one day old. They have learned to drink milk from a bottle.

When a lamb is born, it is covered with soft fleece. As it grows, its woolly coat becomes thick and waterproof. Even in the rain, its curly wool keeps it warm and dry.

Lambs are frisky and playful, but they are easily scared. A lamb will romp across a field, then stop short and run back to its mother. From the day a lamb is born, it follows its mother everywhere. If it gets lost, it calls for her with loud bleats.

Mother goats are called nannies. They usually have twins.

Baby goats are called kids. They look a lot like lambs, but they are much bolder. They often wander away from their mothers. Kids like to climb steep rocks and leap from one rock to another. They're smart too. They can learn to open the latches on farm gates.

The mother and kids on this page are Angora (ang-GOR-uh) goats. They are raised for their long silky hair, called mohair.

This mother and kid are Nubian (NOO-be-un) goats. They are raised for their milk. Goats' milk tastes sweeter than cows' milk.

A mother pig has more babies than any other farm animal. She usually has between eight and twelve piglets at a time. How many piglets can you count here?

The mother is called a sow. Right after she gives birth, the piglets start to make sucking sounds. They crawl through the straw to the sow's nipples. Then they begin to nurse.

Piglets always line up in the same order at feeding time. Each piglet has its own nipple. When the piglets finish nursing, they fall asleep where they are.

These piglets are about a week old. They are big enough to leave their pen and explore the barnyard. When their mother wants them to follow her, she grunts softly.

If you touch a small piglet, it feels like velvet. It is covered with soft, short hairs. When it is about ten days old, it begins to grow stiff bristles.

Baby pigs make lively pets. They will come when you call them and climb into your lap. A pig can be trained to bring the newspaper or pull a cart. It learns some tricks faster than dogs. In fact, pigs are probably the smartest animals on the farm.

A barn is a perfect place for a barn swallow's nest. This swallow has built a nest of mud and straw. All day she flies in and out of the barn door, bringing insects home to her hungry babies. The father swallow brings food too. Baby swallows eat hundreds of insects every day.

In three weeks, young swallows are big enough to fly. The swallow family leaves the barn. It joins a flock of other swallows not far away. When summer ends, all the swallows fly south. Next spring, the mother swallow may return to the same barn to build a new nest.

On most farms, chicken eggs are kept in an incubator (IN-kyuh-BAY-tur) until they hatch. An incubator is a big tray warmed by heat lamps. After the chicks hatch, they can be given to a mother hen. She will adopt them as her own.

These chicks are being raised in the hen house. They're only a day old, but they can already run around and peck for food. When they feel chilly, they cuddle under the mother hen's feathers.

A mother hen talks to her chicks as she leads them around the barnyard. Soft clucking sounds mean "Follow me!" A loud call, *kuk-kuk-kuk-kuk,* means "Here's some food!" A high screech means "Danger! Run for cover!"

Chicks can talk too. When a chick is lost or cold or hungry, it calls for its mother with loud peeps. When it is content, it twitters softly.

This mother goose has made her nest in the corner of a field. She sits on her eggs to warm and protect them. When anyone comes too close, she hisses and beats her wings. She may rush forward and try to bite.

A baby goose is called a gosling. Goslings are ready to leave their nest the day after they hatch. They can walk, run, and feed themselves. Since they are water birds, they can swim too. The goslings follow their mother in a little troop. She leads them to the water. The father goose, called a gander, helps guard the goslings.

After the goslings have a swim, the goose and gander will lead them around the barnyard. Geese are not afraid of other farm animals.

It's hard to imagine a farm without farm dogs. These collie pups are just old enough to leave their mother. They have lots of farm smells to learn about.

Puppies are born blind and deaf. They can barely crawl. They spend all their time nursing and sleeping. When they are three weeks old, they can see and hear. They begin to follow their mother on unsteady legs. At four weeks, the pups are romping and playing.

Collies are found on farms all over the world. They are loyal friends and hard workers. They act as watchdogs. And they help farmers herd sheep and round up cattle.

To a small kitten, a barnyard is an exciting place. This kitten has slipped away from its mother. It is setting out to see the world.

Kittens are as helpless at first as newly born puppies. A kitten starts to purr for the first time when it is a week old. After two weeks, its eyes open. It begins to wet its paws and wash its face. At three weeks it can totter about and follow its mother. It needs its mother's milk and care until it is six weeks old.

A farm cat has a hard time keeping an eye on her kittens. If a kitten wanders too far away, its mother will run to get it. She picks it up by the scruff of the neck and carries it home.

Most farms have cats because they catch rats and mice, which damage crops.

Here's the best mouse-catcher on the farm—a barn owl. The owl is bringing a field mouse home to its young.

A baby owl is called an owlet. Young owlets are always hungry. Their parents hunt at night, when other birds are asleep. A pair of owls may catch as many as twenty mice in a single night.

A barn owl doesn't need a nest. She lays her eggs on the floor of the barn or on a bed of hay. These owlets are still covered with fuzzy down. They won't be able to fly until they are six weeks old. If anyone comes too close, the parents will hiss, screech, and snap their bills. They may even attack with their claws.

This foal is twelve hours old. It was born at night in the stable of a horse farm. The farmer and his family helped it into the world. They cut the cord that tied the foal to its mother. They rubbed the foal dry with towels.

After ten minutes, the foal tried to get to its feet. In half an hour, it was standing by itself. Soon afterwards, it found its mother's milk and began to nurse. Then it lay down in the stable and fell asleep.

In the morning, the foal followed its mother to the pasture. Its knobby legs were still wobbly, but it could already run.

For the next two or three weeks, the foal will grow strong on its mother's milk. Then it will start to nibble at blades of grass. But it will still need milk until it is at least three months old. After that it can live on pasture grass and hay.

The foal already knows its mother by her smell. It feels safe and content by her side. She will watch over her baby as it grows up on the farm.

Index

Index